CHARLES SPURGEON

PREACHING THROUGH ADVERSITY

JOHN PIPER

TABLE OF CONTENTS

A PERSONAL INTRODUCTION

Everyone faces adversity and must find ways to persevere through the oppressing moments of life. Everyone must get up and walk through the routines of making breakfast, and washing clothes, and going to work, and paying bills, and discipling children. We must, in general, keep life going when the heart is breaking.

But it's different with pastors—not *totally* different, but different. The heart is the instrument of our vocation. Charles Spurgeon said, "Ours is more than mental work—it is heart work, the labour of our inmost soul."[1] When a pastor's heart is breaking, therefore, he must labor with a broken instrument. Preaching is the pastor's main work, and preaching is heart work, not just mental work. The question becomes, then, not just how you keep living when the marriage is blank, or when the finances don't reach, or when the pews are bare and friends forsake you; but, *How do you keep preaching?*

---

1 Charles Spurgeon, *Lectures to My Students*, (Grand Rapids: Zondervan Publishing House, 1972), 156.

When the heart is overwhelmed, it's one thing to survive adversity; but then it is something entirely different to continue preaching, Sunday after Sunday, month after month. Spurgeon said to the students of his pastors' college, "One crushing stroke has sometimes laid the minister very low. The brother most relied upon becomes a traitor... Ten years of toil do not take so much life out of us as we lose in a few hours by Ahithophel the traitor, or Demas the apostate."[2] The question for pastors is not, "How do you live through unremitting criticism and distrust and accusation and abandonment?"—but, *How do you preach through it? How do you do heart work when the heart is under siege and ready to fall?*

These are the uppermost questions for many pastors. Preaching great and glorious truth in an atmosphere that is not great and glorious is an immense difficulty. To be reminded week-in and week-out that many people regard your preaching of the glory of God's grace as hypocrisy pushes a preacher not just into the hills of introspection, but sometimes to the precipice of self-extinction. I don't mean suicide.—but something more complex. I mean the deranging inability to know any longer who you are. What begins as a searching introspection for the sake of holiness and humility gradually becomes, for various reasons, a carnival of mirrors in your soul. You look into one and you're short and fat; you look into another and you're tall and lanky; you look into another and you're upside down. Then the horrible feeling begins to break over you that you don't know who you are anymore. The center is

---

2 Spurgeon, *Lectures to My Students*, 161.

not holding. If the center doesn't hold—if there is no fixed "I" able to relate to the fixed "Thou" (namely, God), who is supposed to preach next Sunday?

When the apostle Paul said in 1 Corinthians 15:10, "By the grace of God, I am what I am," he was saying something utterly essential for the survival of preachers in adversity. If, by grace, the identity of the "I"—the "I" created by Christ and united to Christ, but still a human "I"—if that doesn't hold, there will be no more authentic preaching because there is no longer an authentic preacher. When the "I" is gone, there is only a collection of echoes.

O how fortunate are pastors that they are not the first to face these things! I thank God for the healing history of his power displayed in the lives of his saints, and in particular, for the life and ministry of Charles Spurgeon who, for 38 years at the Metropolitan Tabernacle in London, modeled how to preach through adversity.

WHY MIGHT SPURGEON TEACH US?

Throughout the years of my pastoral ministry, I often turned to Charles Spurgeon, and he helped me.

But why? That is the first question to consider. What is it about Spurgeon that makes him such a model saint for modern saints? I offer seven reasons.

1. Charles Spurgeon was a preacher.

Spurgeon preached over six hundred times before he turned twenty years old. His sermons sold about 20,000 copies a week and were translated into twenty languages. Today, his collected sermons fill sixty-three volumes, currently standing as the largest set of books by a single author in the history of Christianity.[3]

Even if his son Charles was biased, his assessment is close enough to the truth: "There was no one who could preach like my father. In inexhaustible variety, witty wisdom, vigorous proclamation, loving entreaty, and lucid

---

3 Eric W. Hayden, "Did You Know?" in *Christian History*, Issue 29, Volume X, No. 1, 2.

teaching, with a multitude of other qualities, he must, at least in my opinion, ever be regarded as the prince of preachers."[4] Spurgeon was a preacher.

2. He was a truth-driven preacher.

We should not be interested in how preachers deal with adversity if they are not first and foremost guardians and givers of unchanging biblical truth. If they find their way through adversity by other means than faithfulness to truth, they will be no help to us.

Spurgeon defined the work of the preacher like this: "To know truth as it should be known, to love it as it should be loved, and then to proclaim it in the right spirit, and in its proper proportions."[5] He said to his students, "To be effective preachers you must be sound theologians."[6] He warned that "those who do away with Christian doctrine are, whether they are aware of it or not, the worst enemies of Christian living... [because] the coals of orthodoxy are necessary to the fire of piety."[7]

Two years before he died he said,

Some excellent brethren seem to think more of the life than of the truth; for when I warn them that the enemy has poisoned the children's bread, they answer "Dear brother, we are sorry to hear

4 C. H. Spurgeon: *Autobiography*, vol. 2, (Edinburgh: The Banner of Truth Trust, 1973), 278.

5 Charles Haddon Spurgeon, *An All Round Ministry*, (Edinburgh: The Banner of Truth Trust, 1960), 8.

6 *An All Round Ministry*, 8.

7 Erroll Hulse and David Kingdon, eds., *A Marvelous Ministry: How the All-round Ministry of Charles Haddon Spurgeon Speaks to us Today*, (Ligonier, PA: Soli Deo Gloria Publications, 1993), 128.

it; and, to counteract the evil, we will open the window, and give the children fresh air." Yes, open the window, and give them fresh air, by all means... But, at the same time, this ought you to have done, and not to have left the other undone. Arrest the poisoners, and open the windows, too. While men go on preaching false doctrine, you may talk as much as you will about deepening their spiritual life, but you will fail in it.[8]

Doctrinal truth was at the foundation of all Spurgeon's labors.

3. He was a Bible-believing preacher.

The truth that drove his preaching ministry was biblical truth, which he believed to be God's truth. He held up his Bible and said,

These words are God's... Thou book of vast authority, thou art a proclamation from the Emperor of Heaven; far be it from me to exercise my reason in contradicting thee... This is the book untainted by any error; but it is pure unalloyed, perfect truth. Why? Because God wrote it.[9]

There is a difference in the hearts of preachers and people where this allegiance holds sway. I once had lunch with a man who bemoaned the atmosphere of his fledging Sunday school class. He said the class typically centered around the group's discussion. One person would raise a

---

8 *An All Round Ministry*, 374.
9 *A Marvelous Ministry*, 47.

topic, and another would find a relevant Bible verse, but then after reading the verse, the attitude became, "Now that we have heard what Jesus thinks, what do you think?" Where that atmosphere begins to take over the pulpit and the church, defection from truth and weakness in holiness are not far behind.

4. He was a soul-winning preacher.

There was not a week that went by in his mature ministry that souls were not saved through his written sermons.[10] He and his elders were always on the "watch for souls" in the great congregation. "One brother," he said, "has earned for himself the title of my hunting dog, for he is always ready to pick up the wounded birds."[11]

Spurgeon was not exaggerating when he said,

I remember, when I have preached at different times in the country, and sometimes here, that my whole soul has agonized over men, every nerve of my body has been strained and I could have wept my very being out of my eyes and carried my whole frame away in a flood of tears, if I could but win souls.[12]

He was consumed with the glory of God and the salvation of men.

5. He was a Calvinistic preacher.

He was my kind of Calvinist. Let me give you a flavor of

---

10 Arnold Dallimore, *Spurgeon*, (Chicago: Moody Press, 1984), 198.

11 *Autobiography*, vol. 2, 76.

12 *A Marvelous Ministry*, 49–50.

why his Calvinism drew 5,000 people a week to his church rather than driving them away. He said,

> *To me, Calvinism means the placing of the eternal God at the head of all things. I look at everything through its relation to God's glory. I see God first, and man far down in the list... Brethren, if we live in sympathy with God, we delight to hear Him say, "I am God, and there is none else."*[13]

> *"Puritanism, Protestantism, Calvinism [were simply]... poor names which the world has given to our great and glorious faith — the doctrine of Paul the apostle, the gospel of our Lord and Savior Jesus Christ."*[14]

But he did make distinctions between the full system of Calvinism, which he did embrace, and some central, evangelical doctrines shared by others that bound him together with them. For example, his favorite was the doctrine of the substitution of Christ for sinners. He said, "Far be it for me to imagine that Zion contains none but Calvinistic Christians within her walls, or that there are none saved who do not hold our views."[15]

He said, "I am not an outrageous Protestant generally, and I rejoice to confess that I feel sure there are some of God's people even in the Romish Church."[16] He chose a paedobaptist to be the first head of his pastor's college, and did not make that issue a barrier to preaching in his

---

13 *An All Round Ministry*, 337.

14 Ibid., 160.

15 *A Marvelous Ministry*, 65.

16 *Autobiography*, vol. 2, 21.

pulpit. His communion was open to all Christians, but he said he "would rather give up his pastorate than admit any man to the church who was not obedient to his Lord's command [of baptism]."[17]

His first words in the Metropolitan Tabernacle, the place he built and in which he preached for thirty years:

I would propose that the subject of the ministry in this house, as long as this platform shall stand and as long as this house shall be frequented by worshippers, shall be the person of Jesus Christ. I am never ashamed to avow myself a Calvinist; I do not hesitate to take the name of Baptist; but if I am asked what is my creed, I reply, "It is Jesus Christ."[18]

But he believed that Calvinism honored that Christ most fully because it was most true. And he preached it explicitly, and tried to work it into the minds of his people, because he said, "Calvinism has in it a conservative force which helps to hold men to vital truth."[19]

Therefore he was open and unashamed: "People come to me for one thing... I preach to them a Calvinist creed and a Puritan morality. That is what they want and that is what they get. If they want anything else they must go elsewhere."[20]

17 *A Marvelous Ministry*, 43.

18 Bob L. Ross, *A Pictorial Biography of C. H. Spurgeon*, (Pasadena, TX: Pilgrim Publications, 1974), 66.

19 *A Marvelous Ministry*, 121.

20 Ibid., 38.

6. He was a hard-working preacher.

I do not look to soft and leisurely men to instruct me how to endure adversity. If the main answer is, "Take it easy," I look for another teacher. Take a glimpse at this man's capacity for work:

> *No one living knows the toil and care I have to bear...*
> *I have to look after the Orphanage, have charge of*
> *a church with four thousand members, sometimes*
> *there are marriages and burials to be undertaken,*
> *there is the weekly sermon to be revised,* The Sword
> and the Trowel *to be edited, and besides all that, a*
> *weekly average of five hundred letters to be answered.*
> *This, however, is only half my duty, for there are*
> *innumerable churches established by friends, with*
> *the affairs of which I am closely connected, to say*
> *nothing of the cases of difficulty which are constantly*
> *being referred to me.*[21]

At his fiftieth birthday, a list was read of sixty-six organizations that he founded and conducted. The Earl of Shaftesbury, a distinguished English title, was present and observed, "This list of associations, instituted by his genius, and superintended by his care, were more than enough to occupy the minds and hearts of fifty ordinary men."[22]

He typically read six substantial books a week and could remember what he read and where to find it.[23] He produced more than 140 books of his own — books like

21 *Autobiography*, vol. 2, 192.
22 Dallimore, *Spurgeon*, 173.
23 "Did You Know?," 2.

The Treasury of David, which was twenty years in the making, and *Morning and Evening*, and *Commenting on Commentaries*, and *John Ploughman's Talk*, and *Our Own Hymnbook*.[24]

He often worked eighteen hours in a day. The missionary David Livingstone, once asked him, "How do you manage to do two men's work in a single day?" Spurgeon replied, "You have forgotten there are two of us."[25] I think he was referring to the presence of Christ's energizing power that we read about in Colossians 1:29 when Paul says, "I toil, struggling with all his energy that he powerfully works within me."

Spurgeon's attitude toward sacrificial labor would not be acceptable today when the primacy of "wellness" seems to hold sway. He said,

> *If by excessive labour, we die before reaching the average age of man, worn out in the Master's service, then glory be to God, we shall have so much less of earth and so much more of Heaven!*[26]

> *It is our duty and our privilege to exhaust our lives for Jesus. We are not to be living specimens of men in fine preservation, but living sacrifices, whose lot is to be consumed.*[27]

Behind this radical viewpoint were some deep biblical convictions that derive from the apostle Paul's teaching.

---

24 Dallimore, *Spurgeon*, 195.

25 "Did You Know?," 3.

26 *An All Round Ministry*, 126–127.

27 Charles Spurgeon, *Lectures to My Students*, 157.

One of these convictions Spurgeon expressed like this: "We can only produce life in others by the wear and tear of our own being. This is a natural and spiritual law—that fruit can only come to the seed by its spending and be spent even to self-exhaustion."[28]

The apostle Paul said, "If we are afflicted, it is for your comfort and salvation" (2 Cor. 1:6). "Death works in us, but life in you" (2 Cor. 4:12). And he said that his own sufferings were the completion of Christ's sufferings for the sake of the church (Col. 1:24).

Another biblical conviction behind Spurgeon's radical view of pastoral zeal is expressed like this:

"Satisfaction with results will be the [death] knell of progress. No man is good who thinks that he cannot be better. He has no holiness who thinks that he is holy enough."[29]

In other words, he was driven with a passion never to be satisfied with the measure of his holiness or the extent of his service (see Phil. 3:12). The year he turned forty he delivered a message to his pastors' conference with the one-word title, "Forward!"[30] In it he said,

In every minister's life there should be traces of stern labour. Brethren, do something; do something; do something. While Committees waste their time over resolutions, do something. While Societies and Unions are making constitutions, let us win souls.

---

28 *An All Round Ministry*, 177.

29 Ibid., 352.

30 Ibid., 32–58.

Too often we discuss, and discuss, and discuss, while Satan only laughs in his sleeve... Get to work and quit yourselves like men.[31]

I think the word "indefatigable" was created for people like Charles Spurgeon.

7. He was a maligned and suffering preacher.

He knew the whole range of adversity that most preachers suffer—and a lot more.

He knew the everyday, homegrown variety of frustration and disappointment from lukewarm members.

[Pastors] understand what one cold-hearted man can do if he gets at you on Sunday morning with the information that Mrs. Smith and all her family are offended, and therefore, their pew is vacant. You did not want to know of that Lady's protest just before entering the pulpit, and it does not help you.[32]

Perhaps even worse, he encountered petty criticisms from those whose support he valued.

What terrible blankets some professors are! Their remarks after a sermon are enough to stagger you... You have been pleading as for life or death and they have been calculating how many seconds the sermon

31 Ibid., 55.
32 Ibid., 358.

occupied, and grudging you the odd five minutes
beyond the usual hour.[33]

It's even worse, he says, if the calculating observer is one of your deacons. "Thou shalt not yoke the ox and the ass together was a merciful precept: but when a laborious, ox-like minister comes to be yoked to a deacon who is not another ox, it becomes hard work to plough."[34]

He also knew the extraordinary calamities that befall us once in a lifetime.

On October 19, 1856 he preached for the first time in the Music Hall of the Royal Surrey Gardens because his own church would not hold the people. The 10,000 seating capacity was far exceeded as the crowds pressed in. Someone shouted, "Fire!'" and there was great panic in parts of the building. Seven people were killed in the stampede and scores were injured.

Spurgeon was twenty-two years old and was overcome by this calamity. He said later, "Perhaps never my soul went so near the burning furnace of insanity, and yet came away unharmed." But not all agreed he was unharmed. The specter so brooded over him for years, and one close friend and biographer said, "I cannot but think, from what I saw, that his comparatively early death might be in some measure due to the furnace of mental suffering he endured on and after that fearful night."[35]

33 Charles Spurgeon, *Lectures to My Students*, 310.

34 Ibid., 311.

35 Darrel W. Amundsen, "The Anguish and Agonies of Charles Spurgeon," in: *Christian History*, Issue 29, Volume X, No. 1, 23.

Spurgeon also knew the adversity of family pain.

He had married Susannah Thomson on January 8 of the same year of the calamity at Surrey Gardens. His only two children, twin sons, were born the day after the calamity on October 20. Susannah was never able to have more children. In 1865 (nine years later), when she was thirty-three years old, she became a virtual invalid and seldom heard her husband preach for the next 27 years until his death. Some kind of rare cervical operations were attempted in 1869 by James Simpson, the father of modern gynecology, but to no avail.[36] So to Spurgeon's other burdens was added a sickly wife and the inability to have more children, though his own mother had given birth to seventeen children.

Spurgeon knew unbelievable physical suffering.

He suffered from gout, rheumatism, and Bright's disease (inflammation of the kidneys). His first attack of gout came in 1869 at the age of thirty-five. It became progressively worse so that "approximately one third of the last twenty-two years of his ministry was spent out of the Tabernacle pulpit, either suffering, or convalescing, or taking precautions against the return of illness."[37] In a letter to a friend he wrote, "Lucian says, 'I thought a cobra had bitten me, and filled my veins with poison; but it was worse— it was gout.' That was written from experience, I know."[38]

So for over half his ministry Spurgeon dealt with ever

---

36 *A Marvelous Ministry*, 38–39.

37 Iain H. Murray, ed., *Letters of Charles Haddon Spurgeon*, (Edinburgh: The Banner of Truth Trust, 1992), 166, note 1.

38 *Letters of Charles Haddon Spurgeon*, 165.

increasingly recurrent pain in his joints that cut him down from the pulpit and from his labors again and again. The diseases eventually took his life at age 57 where he was convalescing in Mentone, France.

On top of the physical suffering, Spurgeon had to endure a lifetime of public ridicule and slander, sometimes of the most vicious kind.

In April, 1855 the Essex Standard carried an article with these words:

> *His style is that of the vulgar colloquial, varied by rant...*
> *All the most solemn mysteries of our holy religion*
> *are by him rudely, roughly, and impiously handled.*
> *Common sense is outraged and decency disgusted. His*
> *rantings are interspersed with coarse anecdotes.*[39]

The Sheffield and Rotherham Independent said,

> *He is a nine days' wonder—a comet that has suddenly*
> *shot across the religious atmosphere. He has gone up*
> *like a rocket and ere long will come down like a stick.*[40]

His wife kept a bulging scrapbook of such criticisms from the years 1855–1856. Some of it was easy to brush off. Most of it wasn't. In 1857 he wrote: "Down on my knees have I often fallen, with the hot sweat rising from my brow under some fresh slander poured upon me; in an agony of grief my heart has been well-nigh broken."[41]

---

39 *A Marvelous Ministry*, 35.

40 Ibid., 35.

41 "The Anguish and Agonies of Charles Spurgeon," 23.

His fellow ministers from the right and left criticized him. Across town from the left Joseph Parker wrote,

Mr. Spurgeon was absolutely destitute of intellectual benevolence. If men saw as he did they were orthodox; if they saw things in some other way they were heterodox, pestilent and unfit to lead the minds of students or inquirers. Mr. Spurgeon's was a superlative egotism; not the shilly-shallying, timid, half-disguised egotism that cuts off its own head, but the full-grown, over-powering, sublime egotism that takes the chief seat as if by right. The only colors which Mr. Spurgeon recognized were black and white.[42]

And from the right James Wells, the hyper-Calvinist, wrote, "I have—most solemnly have—my doubts as the Divine reality of his conversion."[43]

All the embattlements of his life came to climax in the Downgrade Controversy as Spurgeon fought unsuccessfully for the doctrinal integrity of the Baptist Union. In October 1887 he withdrew from the Union. The following January he was officially and publicly censured by a vote of the Union for his manner of protest.[44]

Eight years earlier he had said, "Men cannot say anything worse of me than they have said. I have been belied from head to foot, and misrepresented to the last degree. My good looks are gone, and none can damage me much now."[45]

He gives an example of the kinds of distortions and

---

42 *A Marvelous Ministry*, 69.

43 Ibid, 35.

44 Ibid., 126.

45 Ibid., 159.

misrepresentations that were typical in the Downgrade controversy:

The doctrine of eternal punishment has been scarcely raised by me in this controversy; but the "modern thought" advocates continue to hold it up on all occasions, all the while turning the wrong side of it outwards.[46]

But even though he usually sounded rough and ready, the pain was overwhelming and deadly. In May of 1891, eight months before he died, he said to a friend, "Good-bye; you will never see me again. This fight is killing me."[47]

Spurgeon had recurrent battles with depression.

This final adversity was the result of the others. It is not easy to imagine the omni-competent, eloquent, brilliant, full-of-energy Spurgeon weeping like a baby for no reason that he could think of. In 1858, at age 24, it happened for the first time. He said, "My spirits were sunken so low that I could weep by the hour like a child, and yet I knew not what I wept for."[48]

Causeless depression cannot be reasoned with, nor can David's harp charm it away by sweet discoursings. As well fight with the mist as with this shapeless, undefinable, yet all-beclouding hopelessness... The iron bolt which so mysteriously fastens the door of

---

46 Ibid., 288.

47 "The Anguish and Agonies of Charles Spurgeon," 25.

48 Ibid., 24.

hope and holds our spirits in gloomy prison, needs a heavenly hand to push it back.[49]

He saw his depression as his "worst feature." "Despondency," he said, "is not a virtue; I believe it is a vice. I am heartily ashamed of myself for falling into it, but I am sure there is no remedy for it like a holy faith in God."[50]

In spite of all these sufferings and persecutions Spurgeon endured to the end, and was able to preach mightily until his last sermon at the Tabernacle on June 7, 1891. The question I have asked in reading this man's life and work is, *how did he preserve and preach through this adversity?*

---

49 Charles Spurgeon, *Lectures to My Students*, 163.

50 "The Anguish and Agonies of Charles Spurgeon," 24.

PREACHING THROUGH ADVERSITY

There are innumerable strategies of grace in the life of Charles Spurgeon. The ones I have chosen to mention are limited, and I choose them mainly because they have impacted me personally, but the scope of this man's warfare, and the wisdom of his strategies, were immense.

1. Spurgeon saw his depression as the design of God for the good of his ministry and the glory of Christ.

I begin with the issue of despondency and depression because if this one can be conquered, all the other forms of adversity that feed into it will be nullified. What comes through again and again is Spurgeon's unwavering belief in the sovereignty of God in all his afflictions. More than anything else, it seems, this kept him from caving in to the adversities of his life. He writes,

> *It would be a very sharp and trying experience to me to think that I have an affliction which God never sent me, that the bitter cup was never filled by*

*his hand, that my trials were never measured out
by him, nor sent to me by his arrangement of their
weight and quantity.*[51]

This is exactly the opposite strategy of modern thought, even much evangelical thought, that recoils from the implications of infinity. If God is God he not only knows what is coming, but he knows it *because* he designs it. For Spurgeon, this view of God was not an argument for debate, it was a means of survival.

Our afflictions are the health regimen of an infinitely wise Physician. He told his students,

*I dare say the greatest earthly blessing that God
can give to any of us is health, with the exception of
sickness... If some men, that I know of could only be
favoured with a month of rheumatism, it would, by
God's grace mellow them marvelously.*[52]

He meant this mainly for himself. Though he dreaded suffering and would avoid it, he said,

*I am afraid that all the grace that I have got of my
comfortable and easy times and happy hours, might
almost lie on a penny. But the good that I have
received from my sorrows, and pains, and griefs, is
altogether incalculable... Affliction is the best bit
of furniture in my house. It is the best book in a
minister's library.*[53]

---

51 Ibid., 25.
52 *An All Round Ministry*, 384.
53 "The Anguish and Agonies of Charles Spurgeon," 25.

He saw three specific purposes of God in his struggle with depression. The first is that it functioned like the apostle Paul's thorn to keep him humble lest he exalt himself. He said the Lord's work is summed up in these words:

> *"Not by might nor by power but by my Spirit, saith the Lord." Instruments shall be used, but their intrinsic weakness shall be clearly manifested; there shall be no division of the glory, no diminishing of the honor due to the Great Worker... Those who are honoured of their Lord in public have usually to endure a secret chastening, or to carry a peculiar cross, lest by any means they exalt themselves, and fall into the snare of the devil.[54]*

The second purpose of God in his despondency was the unexpected power it gave to his ministry:

> *One Sabbath morning, I preached from the text, "My God, My God, why has Thou forsaken Me?" and though I did not say so, yet I preached my own experience. I heard my own chains clank while I tried to preach to my fellow-prisoners in the dark; but I could not tell why I was brought into such an awful horror of darkness, for which I condemned myself. On the following Monday evening, a man came to see me who bore all the marks of despair upon his countenance. His hair seemed to stand up right, and his eyes were ready to start from their sockets. He said to me, after a little parleying, "I never before, in my life, heard any man speak who*

---

seemed to know my heart. Mine is a terrible case; but on Sunday morning you painted me to the life, and preached as if you had been inside my soul." By God's grace I saved that man from suicide, and led him into gospel light and liberty; but I know I could not have done it if I had not myself been confined in the dungeon in which he lay. I tell you the story, brethren, because you sometimes may not understand your own experience, and the perfect people may condemn you for having it; but what know they of God's servants? You and I have to suffer much for the sake of the people of our charge... You may be in Egyptian darkness, and you may wonder why such a horror chills your marrow; but you may be altogether in the pursuit of your calling, and be led of the Spirit to a position of sympathy with desponding minds.[55]

The third design of his depression was what he called a prophetic signal for the future.

This depression comes over me whenever the Lord is preparing a larger blessing for my ministry; the cloud is black before it breaks, and overshadows before it yields its deluge of mercy. Depression has now become to me as a prophet in rough clothing, a John the Baptist, heralding the nearer coming of my Lord's richer benison.[56]

I would say with Spurgeon that in the darkest hours it is the sovereign goodness of God that has given me the

---

55 *An All Round Ministry*, 221–222.

56 Charles Spurgeon, *Lectures to My Students*, 160.

strength to go on — the granite promise that he rules over my circumstances and means it for good no matter what anyone else means.

2. Spurgeon supplements his theological survival strategy with God's natural means of survival—his use of rest and nature.

For all his talk about spending and being spent, he counsels us to rest and take a day off and open ourselves to the healing powers God has put in the world of nature. "Our Sabbath is our day of toil," he said, "and if we do not rest upon some other day we shall break down."[57] Eric Hayden reminds us that Spurgeon "kept, when possible, Wednesday as his day of rest."[58] More than that Spurgeon said to his students,

It is wisdom to take occasional furlough. In the long run, we shall do more by sometimes doing less. On, on, on forever, without recreation may suit spirits emancipated from this "heavy clay," but while we are in this tabernacle, we must every now and then cry halt, and serve the Lord by holy inaction and consecrated leisure. Let no tender conscience doubt the lawfulness of going out of harness for a while.[59]

In my pastoral ministry experience, I can testify that time off is crucial for breathing a different spiritual air. When we take time away from the pressure of duty, Spurgeon

---

57 Ibid., 160.

58 Eric W. Hayden, *Highlights in the life of C. H. Spurgeon*, (Pasadena, TX: Pilgrim Publications, 1990), 103.

59 Charles Spurgeon, *Lectures to My Students*, 161.

recommends that we breathe country air and let the beauty of nature do its appointed work. He confesses that "sedentary habits have tendency to create despondency... especially in the months of fog." And then counsels, "A mouthful of sea air, or a stiff walk in the wind's face would not give grace to the soul, but it would yield oxygen to the body, which is next best."[60]

At this point, let me add a personal word to you younger men. In my years of pastoral ministry, I noticed significant changes in my body and soul. They were partly owing to changing circumstances, but much is owing to a changing constitution. First, I had to reduce my calorie-intake to keep from gaining unhelpful weight. During the course of my ministry and aging, my metabolism stopped functioning the same way it once did. Second, I grew to become less emotionally resilient when I didn't get adequate sleep. There were early days when I would work without regard to sleep, and afterwards I would feel energized and motivated. However, as I entered my forties, adequate sleep was no longer a matter of staying healthy, but a matter of staying in the ministry. It is irrational that my future should look bleaker when I get four or five hours sleep several nights in a row, but that point is irrelevant. The fact is that my future felt bleaker, and I must live within the limits of that fact. I commend sufficient sleep to you, for the sake of your proper assessment of God and his promises.

Spurgeon was right when he said,

> *The condition of your body must be attended to... A little more... common sense would be a great gain to some*

---

60 Ibid., 158.

who are ultra spiritual, and attribute all their moods of feeling to some supernatural cause when the real reason lies far nearer to hand. Has it not often happened that dyspepsia has been mistaken for backsliding, and bad digestion has been set down as a hard heart?[61]

3. Spurgeon consistently nourished his soul by communion with Christ through prayer and meditation.

It was a great mercy to me when I discovered John Owen's book, *Communion With God*. Perhaps more than any other, that book nourished me again and again as my soul asked, "Can God spread a table in the wilderness?" Spurgeon warned his students,

Never neglect your spiritual meals, or you will lack stamina and your spirits will sink. Live on the substantial doctrines of grace, and you will outlive and out-work those who delight in the pastry and syllabubs of "modern thought."[62]

I think one of the reasons Spurgeon was so rich in language and full in doctrinal substance and strong in the spirit, in spite of his despondency and his physical oppression and his embattlements, is that he was always immersed in a great book—six days a week. We cannot match that number, but we can always be walking with some great "see-er" of God. Over the years I've learned that the key in all good reading of theology is utterly real fellowship with Christ.

---

61 Ibid., 312.
62 Ibid., 310.

*Above all, feed the flame with intimate fellowship
with Christ. No man was ever cold in heart who
lived with Jesus on such terms as John and Mary did
of old... I never met with a half-hearted preacher
who was much in communion with the Lord Jesus.*[63]

In many ways Spurgeon was a child in his communion
with God. He did not speak in complex terms about anything too strange or mystical. In fact his prayer life seems
more business-like than contemplative.

*When I pray, I like to go to God just as I go to a bank
clerk when I have cheque to be cashed. I walk in,
put the cheque down on the counter, and the clerk
gives me my money, I take it up, and go about my
business. I do not know that I ever stopped in a bank
five minutes to talk with the clerks; when I have
received my change I go away and attend to other
matters. That is how I like to pray; but there is a way
of praying that seems like lounging near the mercy
seat as though one had no particular reason for being
found there.*[64]

This may not be entirely exemplary. It may dishonor the
Lord to treat him like a bank clerk rather than like a moun-
tain spring. But we would make a mistake if we thought that
Spurgeon's business-like praying was anything other than
childlike communion with his Father. The most touching
description I have read of his communion with God comes
from 1871 when he was in terrible pain with gout.

---

63 Ibid., 315.
64 *A Marvelous Ministry*, 46–47.

When I was racked some months ago with pain, to an extreme degree, so that I could no longer bear it without crying out, I asked all to go from the room, and leave me alone; and then I had nothing I could say to God but this, "Thou are my Father, and I am thy child; and thou, as a Father art tender and full of mercy. I could not bear to see my child suffer as thou makest me suffer, and if I saw him tormented as I am now, I would do what I could to help him, and put my arms under him to sustain him. Wilt thou hide thy face from me, my Father? Wilt thou still lay on a heavy hand, and not give me a smile from thy countenance?"... So I pleaded, and I ventured to say, when I was quiet, and they came back who watched me: "I shall never have such pain again from this moment, for God has heard my prayer." I bless God that ease came and the racking pain never returned.[65]

If we are going to preach through adversity, we will have to live in communion with God on such intimate terms— speaking to him our needs and our pain, and feeding on the grace of his promises and the revelations of his glory.

4. Spurgeon rekindled the zeal and passion to preach by fixing his eyes on eternity rather than the immediate price of faithfulness.

The apostle Paul saw that the outer nature was wasting away. And what kept him going was the abiding assurance that this momentary affliction is working for him

---

65 "The Anguish and Agonies of Charles Spurgeon," 24.

an eternal weight of glory. And so he looked to the things that are eternal (2 Cor. 4:16–18). So did Spurgeon.

O brethren, we shall soon have to die! We look each other in the face to-day in health, but there will come a day when others will look down upon our pallid countenances as we lie in our coffins... It will matter little to us who shall gaze upon us then, but it will matter eternally how we have discharged our work during our lifetime.[66]

When our hearts grow faint and our zeal wavers for the task of preaching he calls us to,

Meditate with deep solemnity upon the fate of the lost sinner... Shun all views of future punishment which would make it appear less terrible, and so take off the edge of your anxiety to save immortals from the quenchless flame... Think much also of the bliss of the sinner saved, and like holy Baxter derive rich arguments from the saints' everlasting rest... There will be no fear of your being lethargic if you are continually familiar with eternal realities.[67]

Short of eternity he took the long view when it came to his own persecution. In the Downgrade controversy he said,

Posterity must be considered. I do not look so much at what is to happen to-day, for these things relate to eternity. For my part, I am quite willing to be eaten of dogs for the next fifty years; but the more distant

---

66 *An All Round Ministry*, 76.
67 Charles Spurgeon, *Lectures to My Students*, 315.

future shall vindicate me. I have dealt honestly
before the living God. My brother, do the same.[68]

To keep on preaching in storm of adversity, you must look
well beyond the crisis and feelings of the hour. You must
look to what history will make of your faithfulness, and
most of all, what God will make of it at the last day.

5. For Spurgeon a key to his perseverance in preaching through adversity was that he had settled who he was and would not be paralyzed with external criticism or internal second-guessing.

One of the great perils of living under continual criticism
is that this is a constant call for you to be other than what
you are. This is especially problematic because a humble
saint always wants to be a better person than he is, but
there is a great danger here of losing your bearings in a sea
of self-doubt and not knowing who you are—not being
able to say with Paul, "By the grace of God I am what I am"
(1 Cor. 15:10). Spurgeon felt this danger keenly.

In comparing one ministerial identity with another he
reminded other pastors that at Jesus's last supper there was
a chalice for drinking the wine and there was a basin for
washing feet. Then he said,

I protest that I have no choice whether to be the
chalice or the basin. Fain would I be whichever the
Lord wills so long as he will but use me... So you, my
brother, you may be the cup, and I will be the basin;
but let the cup be a cup, and the basin a basin, and

---

68 *An All Round Ministry*, 360–361.

each one of us just what he is fitted to be. Be yourself, dear brother, for, if you are not yourself, you cannot be anybody else; and so, you see, you must be nobody... Do not be a mere copyist, a borrower, a spoiler of other men's notes. Say what God has said to you, and say it in your own way; and when it is so said, plead personally for the Lord's blessing upon it.[69]

I would also add, plead personally that the Lord's purifying blood be upon it too, because none of our best labors are untainted. The danger, though, is to let fear of man and self-doubt paralyze you from faithfully presenting the truth.

Eleven years later in 1886 he struck the same anvil again:

Friend, be true to your own destiny! One man would make a splendid preacher of downright hard-hitting Saxon; why must he ruin himself by cultivating an ornate style?... Apollos has the gift of eloquence; why must he copy blunt Cephas? Every man in his own order.[70]

Spurgeon illustrates with his own struggle to be responsive to criticism during the Downgrade controversy. For a season he tried to adapt his language to the critics. But there came a time when he had to be what he was.

I have found it utterly impossible to please, let me say or do what I will. One becomes somewhat indifferent when dealing with those whom every word offends. I notice that, when I have measured

---

69 Ibid., 73–74.
70 Ibid., 232–233.

my words, and weighed my sentences most carefully,
I have then offended most; while some of my stronger
utterances have passed unnoticed. Therefore, I am
comparatively careless as to how my expressions may
be received, and only anxious that they may be in
themselves just and true.[71]

If we are to survive and go on preaching in an atmosphere
of controversy, there comes a point where we have done
our best to weigh the claims of our critics and take them
to heart and must now say, "By the grace of God, I am
what I am." We must bring an end to the deranging sec-
ond-guessing that threatens to destroy the very soul.

**6. The strength to go on preaching in the midst of
adversity and setbacks came for Spurgeon from
the assured sovereign triumph of Christ.**

Near the end of his life, around 1890, in his last address at
his pastors' conference, he compares adversity and the ebb
of truth to the ebbing tide.

You never met an old salt, down by the sea, who
was in trouble because the tide had been ebbing out
for hours. No! He waits confidently for the turn of
the tide, and it comes in due time. Yonder rock has
been uncovered during the last half-hour, and if the
sea continues to ebb out for weeks, there will be no
water in the English Channel, and the French will
walk over from Cherbourg. Nobody talks in that
childish way, for such an ebb will never come. Nor

---

71 Ibid., 282–283.

will we speak as though the gospel would be routed,
and eternal truth driven out of the land. We serve
an almighty Master… If our Lord does but stamp
his foot, he can win for himself all the nations of the
earth against heathenism, and Mohammedanism,
and Agnosticism, and Modern-thought, and every
other foul error. Who is he that can harm us if we
follow Jesus? How can his cause be defeated? At his
will, converts will flock to his truth as numerous as
the sands of the sea… Wherefore be of good courage,
and go on your way singing [and preaching!]:

The winds of hell have blown
The world its hate hath shown,
Yet it is not o'erthrown.
Hallelujah for the Cross!
It shall never suffer loss!
The Lord of hosts is with us,
the God of Jacob is our refuge.[72]

---

72 *An All Round Ministry*, pp. 395-396.

꒰꒤꒱ desiringGod

Everyone wants to be happy. www.desiringGod.org was born
and built for happiness. We want people everywhere to understand and embrace the truth that *God is most glorified in us
when we are most satisfied in him.* We've collected more than
thirty years of John Piper's speaking and writing, including
translations into more than 40 languages. We also provide a
daily stream of new written, audio, and video resources to help
you find truth, purpose, and satisfaction that never end. And it's
all available free of charge, thanks to the generosity of people
who've been blessed by the ministry.

If you want more resources for true happiness, or if you want to
learn more about our work at Desiring God, we invite you to visit
us at www.desiringGod.org.

www.desiringGod.org